PRESERVED STEAM
IN DERBYSHIRE

Robert Falconer

HALSGROVE

First published in Great Britain in 2011

British Library Cataloguing-in-Publication Data
A CIP record for this title is available from the British Library

ISBN 978 0 85704 116 6

HALSGROVE
Halsgrove House,
Ryelands Industrial Estate,
Bagley Road, Wellington, Somerset TA21 9PZ
Tel: 01823 653777   Fax: 01823 216796
email: sales@halsgrove.com

Part of the Halsgrove group of companies.
Information on all Halsgrove titles is available at: www.halsgrove.com

Printed and bound by Grafiche Flaminia, Italy

INTRODUCTION

THERE IS SOMETHING ROMANTIC and magical about steam trains, emphasised by films like 'Brief Encounter'. The atmosphere created by steam, smoke and the nostalgia of a bygone age attracts thousands of people who want to ride behind a steam locomotive, take photographs or just experience the unique aroma they create.

You don't have to go far in the UK today to have your own steam experience, and Derbyshire is no exception. Back in the 1960s though, the future of the steam locomotive looked very bleak as British Rail sent them to the scrap yard and replaced them with more modern diesel and electric locomotives.

In the summer of 1968 the age of steam finally came to an end in the UK. On August 11 1968 a special train ran in the northwest for enthusiasts to say farewell. This trip was named 'The Fifteen Guinea' after the price of each ticket. Many enthusiasts were heartbroken by the end of the day, although some steam did keep going on some industrial sites.

Some enthusiasts did not want it to be the end. They decided to do something about it and rallied round to start the new age of steam. A railway revolution grew in strength to save as many locomotives as possible and re-open parts of the railways that had fallen under the Dr Beeching axe.

In 1971, only three years after 'The Fifteen Guinea', steam was once again back on British Rail metals as ex-GWR 'King George V' hauled an enthusiasts' train in the southwest. This would be the first of many more trains to come, with many specials running through Derbyshire.

Through the years there is hardly any part of Derbyshire that has not witnessed the sight of a steam train, from the once railway Mecca of Derby, to Chesterfield and through the dramatic scenery of the Peak District on the Hope Valley line. Buxton and Matlock have also seen occasional trains.

Away from the national network there are a number of preserved lines and centres in Derbyshire. It has always been a dream to re open the spectacular railway line that runs through the Dales in the heart of Derbyshire from Matlock to Buxton. Peak Rail was formed to try and achieve this aim. In the early years they had a small base at Buxton until they moved to the other end of the line and started to operate trains between Northwood and Matlock Riverside through Darley Dale, the station still keeping its original character. From summer 2011 trains were back into Matlock Station regaining a connection to the national network. There is always hard work being done to improve facilities and plans to expand. In 2010 a new engine shed was finished and a turntable opened by Pete Waterman.

Peak Rail runs on the old Midland Mainline from Derby to Manchester, a once very busy and important railway running through the heart of Derbyshire. It was one of the most spectacular lines in the country and a big engineering challenge, requiring tunnels and viaducts to navigate through the Peak District dales. The most famous of the viaducts is the Monsal Head Viaduct which has become a well-known landmark for tourists.

The first part of the line from Ambergate to Rowsley was opened in 1840 and the last steam train to traverse the route was in July 1968. There had been a number of ideas for the line before the chosen route. One of the most ambitious ideas had been to up-grade the Cromford and High Peak line, which would have meant passenger trains on a gradient as steep as 1:8.

One proposed route was to take the railway through Chatsworth Park, but after objections from the Duke of Devonshire a deal was reached with the Duke of Rutland for the line to pass Haddon Hall through a tunnel under the estate. Another idea for the route of the line at the southern end was from Duffield past Wirksworth and construction began. Later there was a change of mind to go through Ambergate to Matlock and Wirksworth became a terminus as part of a downgraded branch line serving the local community and quarries.

The railway to Wirksworth was opened in 1867 but with the increase in road transport the last passenger train ran in 1947. The large volume of stone being quarried from Middlepeak Quarry kept freight trains running until December 1989.

WyvernRail was founded in 1992 with the aim of restoring the line to its former glory, the first goal being achieved in 1996 when they were awarded a Light Railway Order.

It had almost turned to disaster though in 1990 when a track lifting train started work between Idridgehay and Shottle. At the last minute BR management stopped the work when it was thought that there could possibly be new quarry traffic, so the line was mothballed. The quarry trains never did come back but the line was given a better chance of being restored.

In 1997, the Derby and Wirksworth Railway Association was formed in response to growing interest in WyvernRail's activities and was re-named the Ecclesbourne Valley Railway Association in 2000. The Association was converted to a plc in 2002 including a share launch to WyvernRail plc. During this time the steam locomotive 'Whitehead' made a visit to emphasise the railway's ambition of re-opening the route south to Duffield.

2010 has been a landmark year with the first steaming of the Association's own steam locomotive, 'Ferrybridge No.3' built in 1954. In August the newly steamed resident loco was joined by 'Bellerophon', which was built in 1874, for two weekends of steam action. Trains ran south as far as Idridgehay and north on the short steep climb to Ravenstor. The Ecclesbourne Valley Railway is the newest addition to the preserved railway map in Derbyshire and the railway has many plans for the future with more visiting steam locomotives and operating the full length of the line from 2011.

Not too far to the east is another heritage railway, which has been established as the longest in Derbyshire. It is the Midland Railway Centre, which is just north of Ripley.

In 1969, an idea to commemorate the role the Midland Railway had in the industrial history of Derby led to the plan to create a working and static museum about the Midland Railway and its successors. The Midland Railway Project Group helped to support the idea. They were a voluntary labour force which collected and restored exhibits such as semaphore signalling equipment. Two 3F class Jinties Nos. 47327 and 47357 were saved from Barry Scrapyard in Wales. Another one was bought from the National Coal Board.

The Pye Bridge to Ambergate line was closed in 1968 and it seemed a good location for the railway centre. It was not possible to re-open the whole length of the line west of Hammersmith because the line was cut with the building of the A38 and re-alignment of the A610.

The Midland Railway Company was formally launched on the 20 February 1973, changing its name to the Midland Railway Trust in 1976. A huge amount of hard work was needed to restore this railway as Butterley Station, which was to become the headquarters, had been completely demolished. The old main station building from Whitwell, which was identical to the original, was moved and rebuilt on the site.

On 22 August 1981 the first passenger train ran along one mile of track, leaving Butterley at 11.30am. The line was later extended to Ironville and then Pye Bridge. A station was also built at Hammersmith and Swanwick Junction. Signal boxes were moved to the railway including the former Ais Gill Summit box from the famous Settle to Carlisle line.

In recent years there have been big developments at Swanwick Junction with a transport museum, diesel depot, a railway church and a narrow gauge line, which runs into the Golden Valley. Also at Swanwick is the West Shed, which has been the home of the Princess Royal Class Locomotive Trust and their two mighty Stanier Pacifics 'Princess Margaret Rose' and 'Duchess of Sutherland', for many years. One of the most interesting features of the line is between Butterley and Hammersmith where the railway runs across a causeway in the middle of Butterley Reservoir with the train casting a reflection on both sides of the line.

In the northeast corner of Derbyshire is Barrow Hill Roundhouse, the last surviving roundhouse in the UK and a unique example of nineteenth-century railway architecture.

Its construction commenced in July 1869 and was finished in November 1870. The shed code has changed a number of times over the years from M24, 18D, 41E and finally in October 1965 when its doors were closed to steam it was given the code BH.

The shed had been designed to house 24 locomotives but at its peak housed 90 steam engines on the site in the 1920s. The shed's working life ended when it was closed by British Rail in February 1991, a total of 121 years of continuous use.

In 1989 Barrow Hill Engine Shed Society was formed to save the shed, which was by then in decline and was starting to suffer from vandalism.

Hard work took place behind the scenes with the local council to stop the building from being demolished. At the same time British Rail closed the shed it was granted Grade 2 listed status by the Department of the Environment.

The listing came just in time to stop the shed vanishing forever, but it was just the first step. Negotiations with British Rail to buy the buildings started and would take three years. Even though it was now listed Grade 2, it did not stop the vandalism and fear grew that the shed would be destroyed. In 1996 Chesterfield Borough Council became the new owners of the shed and surrounding land.

Work then began to gain funding to restore the site, including repairing major damage to the roof. The dedication of many volunteers came to fruition in July 1998 when the shed was re-opened to the public. Four steam locomotives visited for the occasion with the star of the show being 0-6-0 Johnson 1F No.41708, built in 1880, a former working engine of the nearby Staveley Works and resident at Barrow Hill.

Since then the shed has gone from strength to strength holding very successful galas with many steam locomotives visiting from around the UK such as 'Duke of Gloucester', 'Sir Nigel Gresley' and the newly built 'Tornado'. A number of engines are also housed at the shed on display and the shed is being used as a base to restore engines.

Derbyshire has played an important part in keeping the age of steam alive since 1968 and it will play an important part in the future as preservation societies continue to work hard with staff and volunteers.

Photographing the railways has also become a very popular pastime over the years, trying to capture the romance and atmosphere of the bygone age of rail travel. There are many approaches and styles to photographing steam trains. There is the 'record' type of picture where you stand near to the railway with the sun over your shoulder so the train is fully lit by the sun and you can see all the details in the train. There is also a more 'artistic' approach when often you can't tell what locomotive is in the picture, but the aim is to capture the drama and atmosphere of a steam train. The lighting in these types of pictures can look very beautiful and spectacular as you aim the camera into the sun, creating back light, golden glints on the train and silhouette shapes against the sky.

I have tried to show in this book all the different ways that you can photograph a steam train in all types of weather, including pictures taken at night. You don't have to stand next to a railway to take your pictures; sometimes it can be good to make the train part of a wider landscape. One excellent place in Derbyshire for this is on the Hope Valley Line, which runs through the dramatic Peak District landscape. From Mam Tor you can look down on the train below in Edale, making it look like a toy train as Kinder Scout towers into the sky in the background.

Sometimes we concentrate so much on the steam locomotives that we forget about the people who operate the railways. Focusing on the driver leaning out of the cab or the fireman with his face caked in soot, the guard waving his flag, the signalman pulling the levers in the signalbox or exchanging tokens and the smartly dressed stationmaster, can all add an extra dimension to a photograph.

My first memory of steam trains was when I was three years old in 1976, when my father took me to Leeds Railway Station to see main line specials. At first I was scared of these noisy steam-breathing giants but my initial reaction did not put my father off from taking me many more times to see them.

I soon grew to love trains and it was not long before I envied my father for taking pictures of the steam locomotives. I wanted to do the same and for Christmas 1985 I received my first ever SLR camera, a Pentax S1a. Just two days later I was using the camera to photograph the 'Flying Scotsman' passing through my hometown of Chesterfield. My interest in both steam trains and photography grew and grew.

After leaving school I went on to study photography at college for four years and I have now travelled around the world to China, Cuba, South Africa and USA to see steam.

But it has always been steam action in my home county that has been extra special to me with several great moments over the years. Many of them can be seen in this book.

As well as showing the many different styles of railway photography, this book also shows a large variety of locomotives from the small industrials to large express engines. Many of the world's most famous locomotives have visited Derbyshire, from the replica of 'Rocket', 'Flying Scotsman', 'Oliver Cromwell' to the world's fastest steam loco the 'Mallard'. Also, the most recently-made famous locomotive 'Tornado' has made a few visits to Barrow Hill. This A1 class locomotive has been built from scratch and was first steamed in 2008, the first standard gauge steam locomotive built in Britain since the 1960s. No one travelling on the 'Fifteen Guinea' in 1968 could have imagined what amazing achievements were still to come and instead of steam being confined to the past, it also has a future.

The steam locomotives are undoubtedly the stars of the show but I would like to dedicate this book to the hard working staff and volunteers, whose blood, sweat and tears go into keeping the age of steam alive for thousands of people to enjoy every year.

I would also like to dedicate this book to my father, Michael Falconer. Without his persistence in taking me to see these amazing machines at an early age I would not have developed a keen interest in steam trains and photography, and this book would not have been possible – thank you.

No.6233 'Duchess of Sutherland' passes Stenson Junction en route to Blackpool from Derby in April 2002.

No.4472 'Flying Scotsman' races south from Derby towards Stenson Junction,
seen from a foot crossing in September 1990.

Jubilee class No.45596 'Bahamas' heads north to Derby with the Trent and Mersey Canal in the foreground in May 1989.

A4 class No.4498 'Sir Nigel Gresley' catches the setting sun on the approach to Stenson Junction in March 1989.

No.71000 'Duke of Gloucester' powers south from Derby with its very first mainline
steam special in preservation, with a train bound for Didcot, in April 1990.

No.71000 'Duke of Gloucester' makes a spectacular departure from Derby Station with its second train for Didcot in April 1990.

'Merchant Navy' No.35028 'Clan Line' departs Derby
with a train bound for Didcot in October 1990.

No.3440 'City of Truro' leaves Derby with a train bound for Paddington, London in May 1993.

No.6233 'Duchess of Sutherland' crosses the River Derwent with a train bound for Scarborough from Derby in April 2010. This was the Duchess's first train in preservation in LMS black livery.

No.45596' Bahamas' passes Spondon with a train for Nottingham during a series of shuttles between Derby and Nottingham to celebrate the 'Midland 150' anniversary in June 1989.

No.4965 'Rood Ashton Hall' passes Milford with a train for York in December 2007.

Opposite: No.6233 'Duchess of Sutherland' passes Milford with a train for Scarborough in May 2003.

7F class No.53809 heads south through the Amber Valley near Higham in October 1990.

Opposite: No.6233 'Duchess of Sutherland' passes South Wingfield in the beautiful Amber Valley, heading north in October 2003.

GWR 'Castle' class No.5029 'Nunney Castle' passes Stonebroom just north of Alfreton with a train for York in May 2008.

Opposite: Great Western 'Castle' No.5043 'Earl of Mount Edgcumbe' races
through the snow north of South Wingfield in December 2010.

A4 class No.60009 'Union of South Africa' at Clay Cross Junction with a train for York in October 1996.

No.44767 'George Stephenson' passes Hasland, Chesterfield heading south in May 1993.

8F class No.48151 passes Hasland, Chesterfield with a train for Derby from Buxton in April 1988.

Opposite: No.6233 'Duchess of Sutherland' at Hasland,
Chesterfield, heading south in May 2005.

No.60009 'Union of South Africa' at Hasland, Chesterfield in October 1996.

No.4965 'Rood Ashton Hall' passes Hasland with a train bound for Birmingham in April 2007.

With the 'Crooked Spire' dominating the skyline in the background,
No.4472 'Flying Scotsman' heads south through Chesterfield in December 1985.

The world's fastest steam loco No.4468 'Mallard' passes a more modern generation of speed at Tapton, Chesterfield in May 1988.

No.48151 departs Chesterfield Station with a train for Buxton in October 1987, *photo by Michael Falconer.*

V2 class No.60800 'Green Arrow' crosses over to the Barrow Hill line at Tapton Junction, Chesterfield in June 2001.

'Black 5' class No.5305 is seen light engine at Tapton, Chesterfield in May 1988.

No.45596 'Bahamas' heads north at Chesterfield in May 1989.

No.46203 'Princess Margaret Rose' passes Tapton, Chesterfield in September 1990.

'Black 5' No.5305 is about to cross the Chesterfield Canal at Tapton, Chesterfield in May 1988.
The field on the left-hand side of the picture is now the car park for the Sainsbury's supermarket.

No.44767 'George Stephenson' is in silhouette against the dusk sky on the approach to Tapton heading south in May 1995.

Great Western Hall No.4936 'Kinlet Hall' and No.4953 'Pitchford Hall' cross over the
Chesterfield Canal after visiting Barrow Hill Roundhouse for a gala in October 2006.

LNER locos K1 class No.62005 and K4 class No.61994 'The Great Marquess' cross Chesterfield Canal, heading home from a visit to Barrow Hill Roundhouse in November 2007.

No.70013 'Oliver Cromwell'
climbs past Barrow Hill
in July 2009.

Opposite:
No.5029 'Nunney Castle'
passes Barrow Hill with a
train for York in May 2008.

No.4965 'Rood Ashton Hall' works past Barrow Hill in April 2007.

Opposite: No.6233 'Duchess of Sutherland' passes Barrow Hill with a train for Scarborough from Derby in April 2009.

No.4965 'Rood Ashton Hall' heads away from Barrow Hill,
past Eckington with a train for York in December 2007.

Opposite: A4 Pacific No.60009 'Union of South Africa'
climbs past Barrow Hill in October 1996.

No.5029 'Nunney Castle' approaches Barrow Hill, passing Eckington with a southbound train in May 2008.

No.70013 'Oliver Cromwell'
passes Unstone heading
north to Sheffield in May 2009.

No.5029 'Nunney Castle' makes a fine sight crossing Unstone Viaduct in February 1994.

No.6201 'Princess Elizabeth' passes Dronfield with its support coach, heading north in December 1990.

No.44932 works hard into
Edale in the Peak District
in October 1988.

Opposite:
No.44871 enters Edale
on the Hope Valley Line
in June 2010.

Jubilee class No.5593 'Kolhapur' rests at Edale for a
water stop, with a train bound for Buxton in April 1987.

Opposite: No.45305 works through Edale as Kinder Scout
looms above the train in October 2010.

No.44932 works away from a
water stop at Edale, steaming
valiantly towards Cowburn Tunnel
at the head of the valley
in October 1988.

Opposite:
No.76079 and No.45407
double head past New Mills
heading east in March 2009.

No.76079 and No.45407 head away from New Mills towards Chinley in March 2009.

No.76079 and No.45407 climb towards Chinley with a train for Buxton in October 2007.

In bad weather B1 No.61264 works hard to climb away from Buxton in April 2005.

Opposite: No.44871 climbs past Buxworth with an eastbound train in June 2010.

No.76079 and No. 45407 make a dramatic sight as they depart Buxton
catching the low autumn sun in October 2007.

Opposite: No.5690 'Leander' heads away from Buxton bathed in spring sunshine in April 2006.

No.48151 climbs past Combs in November 1995.

Opposite: No.45407 works hard past Combs on the old LNWR line with
a train for Buxton, surrounded by the beautiful Derbyshire countryside,
just outside Chapel-en-le-Frith in November 2008.

8F class No.48151 recreates a once common sight in Derbyshire at Tunstead Quarry, Great Rocks. It is seen in action for a group of enthusiasts, the day after helping to celebrate the opening of a new hopper loading system in November 1995.

No.48151 is once again in charge of a loaded train, at Tunstead Quarry in November 1995.

Above left: With Riber Castle towering above, No.80080 stands at Matlock Station
in charge of the 'Derwent Explorer' from Nottingham in May 1988.

Above right: Visiting engine 9F class No.92203 'Black Prince' stands at Darley Dale Station, Peak Rail in June 1996.

Visiting 'West Country' class No.34101 'Hartland' departs Darley Dale, Peak Rail on a wet afternoon in May 1995.

Industrial 'Warrington' heads towards Matlock from Darley Dale at Peak Rail in May 1995.

No.1163 'Whitehead' approaches Wirksworth on the Ecclesbourne Valley Railway in April 2002.

No.1163 'Whitehead' arrives at Wirksworth on the Ecclesbourne Valley Railway in April 2002.

Opposite: No.78019 works away from Duffield with a train for Wirksworth in May 2011. No.78019 was brought in from the Great Central Railway to mark the re-opening of the full line from Wirksworth to Duffield.

'Bellerophon' approaches
Shottle from Haywood
with a photographer's charter
at the Ecclesbourne Valley
Railway in August 2010.

Opposite:
Built in 1874 'Bellerophon'
shunts wagons in the
yard at Wirksworth during
a visit in August 2010.

The famous A3 Pacific No.4472 'Flying Scotsman' is seen at Butterley during s short visit in June 1991.

Butterley Station after a heavy snowfall in December 1990.

No.80080 leaves Swanwick
Junction with a train for
Butterley in May 1988.

No.80098 arrives at Swanwick Junction in May 2001.

No.4472 'Flying Scotsman' prepares for a day working on the Midland Railway Centre at Swanwick Shed in June 1991.

Furness Railway No.20, the oldest working standard gauge loco in Britain from 1863, stands at Swanwick Junction Station in May 2001.

The replica of George Stephenson's 'Rocket' gives rides at Swanwick Junction in May 1993.

No.1163 'Whitehead' brings a short goods train off the Swanwick branch at Swanwick Junction in May 2001.

Opposite: Furness Railway No.20 hauls the vintage Midland stock through the
Golden Valley between Pye Bridge and Swanwick Junction in May 2001.

The beautifully restored vintage coaches can clearly be seen as No.20 heads for Swanwick Junction in May 2001.

7F No.53809 is about to depart Hammersmith Station with a 'Santa Special' at the Midland Railway Centre in December 2007.

3F No. 47327 is reflected in
Butterley Reservoir on
1 January 2000.

Opposite:
A tree at the side of
Butterley Reservoir frames
No.47327 in December 2001.

With snow in the fields No.80080 crosses the causeway with a 'Santa Special' in December 1994.

Opposite: Caprotti standard No.73129 crosses Butterley Reservoir, with a 'Santa Special' in December 2007.

The low December sun illuminates No. 80098 in 2004.

Opposite: No.73129 creates a perfect reflection as the winter sun catches the train in February 2006.

With the lake completely frozen under snow and ice No.73129 departs
Butterley and starts to cross the causeway in December 2010.

No.47357 crosses very still waters bathed in golden light in December 2003.

No. 80080 heads across the reservoir with a train for Hammersmith in December 1997.

No.45596 'Bahamas' runs round its train at Hammersmith as the sun shines on the water in September 1992.

No.44932 leaves Hammersmith with a 'Santa Special' in December 1990.

No. 47327 creates a silhouette against the dusk sky on 1 January 2000.

No.46203 'Princess Margaret Rose' crosses Butterley Reservoir against the sun's after glow in December 1994.

A close up detail of 'Jubilee'
No.45593 'Kolhapur' inside
Barrow Hill Roundhouse.

Opposite:
No.73129 heads into the sunset
on Christmas Eve 2008.

A trio of former LMS locos enter the main yard at Barrow Hill Roundhouse in July 1999. 4F class No.44422 leads the way followed by 8F No.48141 and 'Jubilee' No. 45993 'Kolhapur'.

Southern pair 'Beattie' tank No.30587 and 'Terrier' No. 662 'Martello' are in charge of a vintage coach on the short branch line at Barrow Hill Roundhouse in August 2008.

Surrounded by autumn tints, J15 class No. 65462 is in charge of a small goods train along the branch line at Barrow Hill in November 2007.

'Tornado', 'Blue Peter' and 'Sir Nigel Gresley' are bathed in spring sunshine
in their early British Rail liveries in April 2009.

Opposite: A spectacular sight of LNER Pacifics in the yard at Barrow Hill Roundhouse in April 2009.
From left to right are A1 class No.60163 'Tornado', A2 class No.60532 'Blue Peter',
A4 class No.60007 'Sir Nigel Gresley' and A4 No.60009 'Union of South Africa'.

No.4936 'Kinlet Hall' stands on the main line connection line at Barrow Hill Roundhouse after bringing in a mainline steam special from Birmingham in October 2006.

The streamlined profile of A4 No.60007 'Sir Nigel Gresley' can
clearly be seen in the yard at Barrow Hill in April 2009.

B12 class No.61574 stands just outside Barrow Hill Roundhouse in July 2001.

Midland 1F No.41708, once resident at Barrow Hill works a short goods train in the yard, including two wagons originally from just down the road at Clay Cross in July 2001.

'Tornado' stands in the foreground in the yard. K1 No. 62005 and No.60007 'Sir Nigel Gresley' can be seen in the background in April 2009.

With a Great Western flavour in the yard at Barrow Hill 'Castle' No.5051 'Drysllwyn Castle' now named 'Earl Bathurst' stands on the left alongside 'Manor' No.7822 'Foxcote Manor' in July 2003.

The yard at Barrow Hill is full of Great Western locos in July 2003, with 'Foxcote Manor'
and 'Drysllwyn Castle' dominating the foreground.

An LNER flavour in Barrow Hill yard in November 2007. On the left is V2 class No.4771
'Green Arrow', then A2 No.60532 'Blue Peter' and B1 class No.1306 'Mayflower'.

J15 No. 65462 catches the autumn sun in the yard at Barrow Hill in November 2007.

On a glorious summer's evening in July 2001 B12 No. 61574 works a goods train
on the branch line past 'Austerity' No.68005, Y7 No.68088 and 1F No.41708.

No.61574 and No.68005 turn to gold as the sun starts to set in July 2001.

Barrow Hill yard is full of atmosphere on a summer evening in July 2001.

A yard full of locomotives, stand out against a dramatic sunset at Barrow Hill in July 2002.

The warm light from the
setting sun shines into
Barrow Hill Roundhouse
and highlights 8F No.48151,
which takes centre stage in
the picture in July 2000.

A very atmospheric scene inside Barrow Hill Roundhouse in July 2000, a sight which was once a common sight up and down the country.

The crew of Y7 class No.68088 are outlined against the sunset in the yard at Barrow Hill in July 2001.

Former Lancashire &
Yorkshire 'Pug' No.51218
takes water outside Barrow Hill
Roundhouse in July 2000.

Standing in the night air in the yard at Barrow Hill Roundhouse are LNER engines
V2 No.60800 'Green Arrow' and B1 class No.61264 in April 2002.

The outline of two A4 Pacifics can be seen in the yard in April 2009. On the left is No.60007 'Sir Nigel Gresley', alongside No.60009 'Union of South Africa'.

The silhouette of 1F No.41708, once resident at Barrow Hill,
can be seen inside the Roundhouse on the re-opening day in July 1998.

No.41708 stands on the turntable facing 4F class No.44422 re-numbered No.44483 and 3F class No.47383 changed to 47630 in July 1998.

Barrow Hill Roundhouse is filled with locomotives in July 2001. Left to right are 'Austerity' No.68005, 'Crab' class No.42700, 1F No.41708, 9F class No.92203 'Black Prince' re-numbered No.92206 and Y7 class No.68088.

No.48151 receives some oil inside Barrow Hill Roundhouse in July 2000.

135

Standing majestic around the turntable in April 2002 are V2 No.60800 'Green Arrow',
B1 No.61264 re numbered No.61238 and 'Jubilee' No.45593 'Kolhapur'.

Opposite: No.41708 stands under the impressive roof of Barrow Hill Roundhouse
in July 1998, just after the completion of the restoration.

Barrow Hill Roundhouse was filled with Great Western engines in
July 2003 with Nos.5637, 5224 and 5553 taking centre stage in the picture.

In November 2007 the Roundhouse had an LNER flavour with B1 No.61264, K4 class
No.61994 'The Great Marquess' and J15 class No.65462 positioned around the turntable.

B1s No.1306 'Mayflower' and No.61264 look on as J15 class No.65462 stands on the turntable in November 2007.

A pair of B1s stand together in steam for the first time in preservation in
November 2007 with No.61264 on the left and No.1306 'Mayflower' on the right.

The crew find time for a chat as B12 class No.61574 stands
inside Barrow Hill Roundhouse in July 2001.

An elevated view inside Barrow Hill Roundhouse full of atmosphere in November 2007.

'Merchant Navy' class No.35005 'Canadian Pacific' simmers in the night air in the yard at Barrow Hill in July 1999.